THINK LIK
THE MANUFACTU**R**ER S SELLING EDGE

SETTING
The
TABLE

THE VITAL POINTS SALES REPS NEED TO KNOW
WHEN SELLING TO THE RETAIL INDUSTRY.

BUCK JONES

Copyright © 2018 Buck Jones.

All rights reserved. No part of this book may be reproduced, stored, or transmitted by any means—whether auditory, graphic, mechanical, or electronic—without written permission of both publisher and author, except in the case of brief excerpts used in critical articles and reviews. Unauthorized reproduction of any part of this work is illegal and is punishable by law.

ISBN:1986966267
ISBN-13:9781986966269

CONTENTS

I   The Most Important Chapter in the Booklet............................1

II   Do You Practice These Six Critical Points? 7

III   The One Point You Must Convince Your Retailer..................17

IV   Why You Must Make it About Your Retailer,
        & Not About You 23

V   Why Piling Up the Benefits is Essential 33

VI   What Values Do You, Personally Add? 43

VII   Are There Times When You Shouldn't Be Selling?.................57

Final Thoughts...65

About the Author 67

CHAPTER I

THE MOST IMPORTANT CHAPTER IN THE BOOKLET

Hi Guys, my name is Buck Jones, I've been doing this a long time, and I guess in many ways, I'm just like you. The only difference is, I came up through the retail side of this business while most of you came up through the manufacturing side. Maybe the only other point is that I'm probably a little older than you, which has given me the chance to spend a good part of the last decade working with manufacturer sales reps and retail accounts all across this country.

The reason this booklet is even in existence, is because through all of this work, two consistent facts keep coming up. These are …

… most sales reps I've met, have very little understanding of the retailer side of the business, … they really don't understand who they are selling to, … and …

… once salespeople begin to understand more about their retailers' needs, their sales presentations become more aligned with these needs, and that results in increased sales.

Now, of course, I don't know you personally. I don't know how well you, … align with your retail clients, … work to build win-win presentations, … or what your retailers think of you. But I do know this, …

> … research shows retailers rate less than 20% of the sales people they see as 'Good' or 'Excellent' at their jobs.

> … sales people often think their presentation or proposal is 'in the game,' when in reality, the retailer has thrown them out of the ballpark, and they don't even know it

> … most sales people can't tell me what 'really has to happen or occur' in order for their retailer to say yes to their proposal

> … and finally, most manufacturing companies think they're selling products or services to the retailer, and have no idea how far off base that thinking really is

But, don't get me wrong, I'm not going to tell you how to sell. I'm not a salesperson, … that was never my job and I don't intend to start now. I'm a retailer! I think like a retailer, talk like a retailer and act like a retailer. And, the good news is, because you've already got this booklet, you don't have to take me out to lunch or work at my new store's Grand Opening to get it. *(See, I really was a retailer.)*

Instead, I'm just going to give you a quick look at a small part of the retail side of the business, … how we think *(Yes, we do think)*, …. what's important to us, … and some of the reasons we say 'yes' or 'no' to your proposals.

Basically, this is just me, talking with you. And, I believe the 'key' to you being a better salesperson, is for you to become better at using your products and services to provide what I, as a retailer, want. You see, for me, you understanding more about what I want and need is helpful to both sides, … retailer and manufacturer.

I believe in the old saying, …

…a deal can always be made when both parties see their own benefit in making it.

This saying goes right to the heart of what I'm hoping you begin to grasp from this booklet. So …

… if, by explaining what retailers are looking for, I can help salespeople design programs that benefit me, as a retailer, as well as them, then we're both way ahead of the game."

And, as I said, I won't tell you how to sell, but I will tell you what I was thinking (and what retailers I work with today are usually thinking) in these selling circumstances, … AND, … I can share with you what I would do if I WERE trying to get ME to buy more of your products.

That's all this is, … me sharing with you what I would do if I were trying to sell to ME.

And, as always, you have a choice, … you can accept what I'm sharing, or you can dismiss it, … it's just that simple. But just so you know, as I came up through the retail hierarchy I held almost every retail position from store manager to Vice President, so I've been in the position of the person sitting on the opposite side of the desk from you in almost every retail buying circumstance you can imagine.

I've been there, and I'm working with retailers who are in those exact same situations today. So thanks for reading this, … get ready, … and have fun with these ideas!

Oh, and in case you haven't figured it out yet, this is more of an INTRODUCTION, than a real 'Chapter 1.' I thought if you knew it was the 'Introduction,' you wouldn't read it, after all, hardly anybody looks at an 'Introduction.' So by just titling it this way, I thought I'd have a better chance of getting you to read it. *(Yes, we retailers can be sneaky.)* So, if you did, it worked. SURPRISE!

QUESTIONS:

(Fill in the Blank) Research shows retailers rate less than _____% of the sales people they see as 'Good' or 'Excellent' at their jobs.

In this chapter, a comment is made that sales reps often think their presentation is "in the game," when in reality, the retailer has thrown them out of the ballpark. Has this ever happened to you? If so, how did you discover it? How did it make you feel?

_____

_____

_____

_____

_____

_____

Buck makes the comment, in this chapter, that something has to 'happen or occur' in order for a retailer to say 'yes' to your proposal. Do you know what this is? If you do, list it here.

_____

_____

_____

_____

_____

_____

In this chapter, Buck also comments that most manufacturing companies think they're selling products and services, but this is far off base. If that's the case, then what are manufacturing companies selling?

_____

_____

_____

_____

_____

_____

CHAPTER **II**

DO YOU PRACTICE THESE SIX CRITICAL POINTS?

Look, as we begin this journey, there are half-a-dozen things about the retail side of the business, which I need to explain. You probably know most of these anyway, but it never hurts to reinforce something you may already know.

1. Your Selling Objectives Need To Change Based On The Title of Your Retail Contact

In every retail organization, the responsibilities vary from one title, or job description, to another. Typical retail job titles include: Store Manager, District Manager, Buyer, Director, Category Manager, Vice President, Executive Vice President, etc.

Each of these positions, and therefore the people holding those titles, has certain responsibilities. Their annual reviews and bonuses depend on how well they handle those responsibilities and the objectives that go with them.

Therefore, the needs and problems of a store manager, are different from the needs and problems of a buyer, which are different from a director, which are different from a VP, and on and on.

So, if you're trying to sell to a buyer, you need to concentrate on the benefits that help that buyer. If you're working with a Category manger, concentrate on the benefits that help the category manager. Be sensitive to the needs and objectives of each retail person you deal with, ... and above everything else, ...

... don't assume just because your retail contact isn't interested in a particular benefit, that other people within the company aren't.

That would be a big mistake.

2. As a Corporate Buyer, I See Sales Reps All Day Long

Okay, if I'm a retail buyer, I'll see a minimum of 5 to 6 salespeople every day, and in some companies it will be a lot more. That translates into seeing a minimum of 25 to 30 salespeople per week, and in 50 fifty weeks I'll have had 1,250 to 1,500 sales meetings. Wow, that makes me tired just thinking about it.

So, if for no other reason than these numbers, it doesn't take long before I can become quite good at this sales and negotiating game. I do it all the time, over and over. But it also means, by the time you walk into my office, I've probably already ...

- ... had 2 or more presentations today before you, and I'll have another 2 or more after you leave

- ... heard most every 'sales pitch' there is trying to get more 'space'

- ... said "No" to more than a dozen proposals this week alone

- … just had your biggest competitor in my office telling me how great their proposal is for my company

So, when you walk in my door, I want to know, …

...what is it about you, that says I should give you more time and pay more attention to you, than any of the other 29 people I'll see this week?

You see, this is the question I'm trying to answer as you come into my office and sit down in front of me. And of course the other point is, if you can't answer that question, how do you expect me to?

3. When I First Meet You, I Consider You A Slug!

I'm your new salesman from ABC Foods!

Research shows retailers rate only 20% of the salespeople they see as 'Good' or 'Excellent' at their job. That means 4 out of every 5, or 80%, of the people I see each week don't even make the 'good' rating. I've always had a name for them, … I call them 'slugs.' That's right 'slugs.' I call them that because they just seem to 'slide in' and 'slide out.' Plus, sometimes they even leave a nasty trail, … of course, that only happens with the real bad slugs.

But, here's my point, if 80% of the sales people I see throughout the year are 'Slugs,' and you're a new salesperson just assigned to my company, … what do the odds tell me you are? That's right, what do the odds say you are?

You see, without knowing anything about you, the odds tell me you're a slug, too.

And quite honestly, from my perspective, I have no choice but to consider you a slug until you prove to me that you're different.

4. Ask More Questions

One of the biggest mistakes most sales reps make, is not asking enough right questions. Look, the main way to find out about your retailer's objectives, problems and/or goals, is to ask. So, if you truly want to help me, as your retailer, then you have to know what I need, what benefits I'm looking for, and what problems I'm trying to solve. But, if 80% of the people I see are slugs, why would I open up and talk with you? Therefore, you're going to have to build some common ground, and then you're going to have to ask.

The other key here is, you have to make sure and "ask the RIGHT questions." You see, as a general rule, never ask a retailer a question that you should know or can find out the answer, for yourself. For example, NEVER ask questions like …

- " … how many stores do you have?"

- " … what kind of displays do you use in your lobby?"

- " … do you use display tables up front?"

- " … how often do your ads come out?"

When you ask these type of questions, all you're doing is reinforcing how little you actually know, and how little effort you've put into finding out about my business.

One other very important point here, ... never ask your question without giving something to the retailer BEFORE you actually ask the question. That's right, make sure to give something before you ask for something back. As an example, here's a question the way most salespeople would ask it ...

"Are you making any changes in your strategy to address your customer's health concerns?"

This is a one-way question. If the retailer responds and answers the question, information is only flowing one-way, ... from the retailer to you. That's not good. You will find you'll have much more success if you ask the question more like this ...

"Research is telling us that 75% of today's consumers are trying to eat healthier. Because of that, we're looking to manufacture some new product lines in our company. Are you guys seeing the same situation and what kind of changes are you making in your strategy because of it?"

Do you see the difference? Here we give out information (75% of today's consumers are trying to eat healthier, ... and ... we're looking to manufacture some new product lines) BEFORE we actually ask the retailer the question we want answered.

Asking more questions is a key to building a solid relationship with your retailer, ... but what questions you ask, AND how you ask them are critical elements to how successful you actually will be.

5. Dialogue versus Monologue

Okay, here's a fact, … that's right, a FACT, …

> ### … over 90% of the sales reps out there today, love to hear themselves talk.

Okay! Okay! Maybe this really isn't a fact, but it sure seems once they get going, it's hard to get them to stop! Now, don't get me wrong, I understand why this happens. After all, you've …

- … finally got you're appointment with me

- … gathered all of your information together

- … been preparing your presentation

- … only have 30 minutes to get it all in

Then **"BANG,"** you're there, and off you go! It's almost like you've got all of these things you want to say, bottled up inside, you're a little nervous and then you start and WHAM!, here it all comes.

But here's the problem, … you do NOT want this to be a "here's what I have, … isn't it great? … it does this and that, … it comes packed like this, … customers think this and that, … and it took us this long to develop it" kind of presentation. Then you end your lecture with the "so, what do you think?" comment.

Now, you may think I'm kidding, but I see this all of the time. In fact, as recently as last week, during a simulation with a company I work with, I had a saleswoman actually get 15 minutes into her presentation before ever asking me one single question. She had so much she wanted to say, and she just got going, so I didn't stop her. I just sat there and let her go on, and on and on.

Plus, as I'm sure most of you know, if you don't get your retailer engaged, it's easy for them to get distracted, not pay attention, and instead, they just end up waiting for you to finish so they can escort you out the door. Of course, the game was over long before you finished, you just never realized it.

So honestly, you'll do much better if you work to make your 30 minute appointment a dialogue, between the two of you with questions, answers and information flowing back and forth. You'll need to take control and lead it, but fight to stay away from that monologue mentality. Develop your DIALOGUE skill and you'll be amazed how it will improve all aspects of your selling relationships.

6. It's Usually About Space

Okay, I can't say <u>every</u> sales presentation that was ever made asked for more space, but (1) I bet at least 95% of them did, … and (2) I definitely know I've never had a manufacturer ask for less space. Everybody wants another product facing or two, an extra display, or a table or rack stocked with their product. So, if you're looking for more space, and you're convinced there's no way I can say 'no' to your proposal because it's the best thing I'll ever see *(that was sarcastic, in case you didn't know)*, you need to come up with a plan.

In other words, when it comes to 'space,' I honestly believe I don't have any more. So you'll have a much better chance to get me to say 'yes' if you can show me that there is space available to implement your proposal. That means you have to take it upon yourself to get in my stores, check out where you think there's room for your proposal, and then be able to show me how that can apply in all of my stores.

So, in this "Lay the Foundation" chapter, here are the six points I wanted to present to you before we got too far along:

1. Your Selling Objectives Need To Change Based On The Title of Your Retail Person

2. As a Corporate Buyer, I See a Minimum of 5 to 6 People a Day, You're Just One of Many

3. When I First Meet You, The Odds Tell Me You're A Slug!

4. Ask More Questions, But Make Them The Right Questions

5. Use A Dialogue, Not A Monologue

6. Find The 'Space' Before You Ask For It

QUESTIONS:

On the proceeding page, Buck lists his six important points to "Lay the Foundation" for the rest of this booklet. Which one, of those points, do you regard as the most important and why?

_____

_____

_____

_____

_____

What do you think is the basic difference between a 'Right Question,' and a 'Wrong Question?' Do you agree with this concept?

_____

_____

_____

_____

_____

What's the basic difference between a Monologue and a Dialogue? Why should this make a difference when you're making your presentation?

_____

_____

_____

_____

_____

In this chapter Buck says when he first meets you, the odds tell him you're a SLUG! What is a Slug? Why do the odds tell him that? What must you do so you're not regarded as a Slug any longer?

_____

_____

_____

_____

_____

CHAPTER **III**

THE ONE POINT YOU MUST CONVINCE YOUR RETAILER

For me, and most of the retailers I work with today, one of, if not the most important characteristic for building a trusted business relationship, is …

… making me believe you truly care about my business and honestly want to help.

You see, if I feel this way about YOU, then a couple of things happen, … (1) I really will try to find ways to use YOUR products and (2) even when things get tough, and sooner or later they always do, I'll try to find ways to keep YOU in the game.

Of course, what we're talking about here is much more personal than just the products you have and that particular promotion you're trying to get me to buy this month. This is about YOU, and how I feel about YOU, … and as far as business is concerned, it's as personal as it can get.

So why is this type of relationship so important? Don't forget, retailers rank only 2 out of 10 salespeople as doing a 'good' or 'excellent' job (*I actually think that number is high*), … while the rest are regarded more as 'order takers' who are only concerned about what THEY can get out of a deal. So imagine how different it is to find salespeople who are not just interested in what THEY can get out of me, ... or what kind of business THEY can do, ... but also realize the importance of helping me build MY business?

Now this is an ally type of business relationship, one where we look to build both of our businesses, instead of the normal adversarial type of business where we're on opposite sides of the desk each one trying to get as much as possible from the other.

Now, I'm not as naive as you may think, ... so yes, I've always understood that, ...

... I have no way of really knowing how these sales reps actually felt, or what they said after they left my office.

As far as I know, they could have walked out my door, called home immediately, and ranted to their spouse about what a terrible person or idiot I was.

But, as far as I ever knew (and this is what's important), and based on everything I ever heard or saw from them, there was nothing that ever led me to believe other than they actually did care about my business."

Plus, they demonstrated this give and take relationship throughout our dealings together by being willing to sacrifice a little now and then from their own goals and objectives knowing I would do the same for them later on down the line, ... and I did.

So how does this all happen? What has to take place before this kind of relationship can actually exist? How do you show you truly care about your retailer and sincerely want to help? Well, for me it came down to three basic points: Personal Desire/Attitude, Personal Ability, and Company Ability. Here's what I mean.

- First, **PERSONAL DESIRE/ATTITUDE**: Are you the kind of person who truly wants to help me? In other words, I'm trying to determine if YOU truly care about what happens to MY business, not just YOURS? I need to know this. And, yes, everyone will say they are, but that's just not the case. Plus, this can be a slippery slope, because I know your job is to gain as much access to my customers as you can. But, I've always found it's where and how you draw the lines between what's good for YOU, and what's good for ME, that really determines this issue. And, I'm always watching and evaluating how you make those judgments.

- Second, **PERSONAL ABILITY**: Do I believe you're truly capable of helping me? You see, everyone 'says' they want to help, BUT do you really know enough about your own products and services, ... my industry, ... my company, ... and my team and me, to offer good solid business opinions? Are you knowledgeable? Are you dependable? Are you trustworthy? In short, are you the kind of person I'd want as a business partner? You see, that's what I'm really trying to assess.

- And third, **COMPANY ABILITY**: Do you represent enough business where you can actually make a difference? You see, you might want to help, you might even be knowledgeable enough to help, but you might represent such a small amount of business that there's really no benefit to me, one way or the other.

I often make this point by talking about a mustard salesman I once  knew who called on me years and years ago. He sold mustard, and it was good mustard, and I mean, really good mustard. He had two sizes, an 8 oz. bottle and a 12 oz. bottle. Now I liked this salesman, he was honest, professional, and he was always trying to find ways to help me. The problem was, he sold mustard, … just mustard, and it only came in two different sizes.

So truthfully, no matter what program he came up with, no matter what merchandising idea or great marketing concept he developed, the benefits he could provide me were very limited. In fact, there was no way he could really affect my business or help me reach any of my objectives. I mean, even if we tripled his mustard business tomorrow morning, it wouldn't have made a ripple toward my sales goals. So, as far as trying to form a business partnership together, where we both were trying to build each other's business, it couldn't work because he really couldn't provide me any measureable benefits.

Now, does that mean we didn't do business together, or weren't friends? Not at all, in fact, we're still in contact today. But from a business perspective, I only have a certain amount of time. And, since my company pays me to care about them, I have to spend my time and effort where I can get the best benefits for my company.

So, it's important all of these points are in place. I need to believe: you truly **WANT** to help me, that you have the **ABILITY** to help me, and that you represent enough sales that you actually **CAN** help me. If these criteria are in place then we have the opportunity to build a solid business relationship that can become a WIN-WIN for both of us. Now those are the kind of business relationships retailers are looking to form!

QUESTIONS:

What does Buck say is, "one of, if not the most important characteristic, a sales reps must portray, if desiring to build a trusted business relationship with a retailer?" Do you agree? Why or why not?

_____

_____

_____

_____

_____

_____

In this chapter, Buck lists three basic points that he needs to feel are in place, in order for a truly reciprocal business relationship to develop. List those three points and briefly explain why they are important.

1. _____

_____

_____

_____

_____

2. _____

_____

_____

_____

_____

3. _____

_____

_____

_____

_____

CHAPTER **IV**

WHY YOU MUST MAKE IT ABOUT YOUR RETAILER, & NOT ABOUT YOU

I remember how excited I was during my first few days as a new buyer. I had accepted a job with a new company and was advancing up from the stores to the corporate office. I was really looking forward to this whole new experience and was excited about the possibilities.

My job description called for a 5 1/2 day work week. Mondays were used for planning and getting things set (warehouse deliveries, allocations, ad programs). Then I'd spend Tuesday thru Friday morning seeing salespeople, getting my ads together and attending company meetings. And finally, Friday afternoons and Saturday mornings I'd be in the stores.

Now obviously things changed each week, but this was my official schedule and as you can see, a good amount of my time, especially Tuesday through Friday, was spent listening and listening and listening to salespeople. *(Believe me, once sales people get talking it's hard to get a word in, so I could only listen)* Now, as a store manager, I had salespeople calling on me, so it wasn't like this was a new experience, but what surprised me, was how predictable and self-absorbed so many of these 'corporate' salespeople were.

Each Tuesday morning it would start. I would be at my desk and one after another they would come in, sit down in front of me, hand me the deal sheet they filled out while waiting to see me and then start talking about what product they had for me to buy.

I'd sit there and listen to ...

> ... *"this week, <u>WE'VE</u> reduced our item $5 per case,"* or

> ... *"this month <u>WE'RE</u> promoting ..."* or

> ... *"for the next six weeks <u>WE'VE</u> got this on special ..."* and on and on it would go.

Even if they had a new item, they would still continue with comments like, *"it ...*

> ... *has been in development for more than 4 years"*

> ... *comes in 8oz. bags, packed 24 per case"*

> ... *is projected to deliver sales increases of almost 10% over its 4-week intro period"*

> ... *comes in three delicious flavors"*

> ... *has an advertising budget of over $24 million"*

> ... *will be featured in MLB ads throughout next summer"*

> ... *had great retail shopper test results"*

To me, these guys were nothing more than 'deal sloggers' or 'order takers.' One after another they paraded through my office. And I guess what amazed me, was rarely, if ever, did I get asked about OUR goals, or about what we were trying to accomplish, or what we were interested in. It was never about ME or MY company, ... instead, I just got a continual dose of what THEIR company had put on deal or the promotion THEY were featuring. That was it, day after day, ... week after week. And you have no idea how many times, after a salesperson left my office, I'd just take their deal sheet and file it in that big wide-mouth circular file under my desk! They're gone! Done with that one! Next!

...and WE'VE got this on special,
... WE'VE reduced our top item $5 per case,
... WE'RE promoting a, ... and WE think this ... !

This was my introduction to corporate retail buying and selling, ... this was my introduction to corporate supplier sales reps, ... this was my introduction to broker sales reps, ... and this was my introduction to what I've seen over and over ever since, ... salespeople who seem only to be interested in **THEIR** items, **THEIR** programs and **THEIR** sales.

Now look, I'm not saying that's the way you are, ... after all, I don't even know you, but I do know the industry is filled with sales people who ARE that way. So here's a point I'd like you to consider.

My retail company doesn't pay me to care about you. And they don't pay me to care about what item you've got on special or some company promotion your marketing team put together. Instead, my company pays me to care about them, ... MY Company. Okay? Good!

Now, since that's the truth, here's one simple question ...

**If it's true that my company is paying me to care
about them, why then, would I be
interested in something you've got, unless
it benefits MY company and ME?**

I mean, just think about this for a minute or two. Why would I be interested in something you've got, unless it's a benefit to US. And subsequently, if you want me to pay attention to what you're saying, … if you want me to consider what you're saying as a possible program I could use, … then shouldn't you concentrate on the points of your program that explain all of the benefits I'll receive or gain if I use it?

I mean, shouldn't you be telling me all of the reasons why your proposal will help **ME** and **MY COMPANY**? Look, one of the most important truths about retailers is this, …

Retail Buyers don't purchase products or services, … **we purchase what we think those products or services will give us or do for us.**

Wow, this is really, really, important. Retail buyers don't purchase products or services, … they purchase what they think those products or services will give them or do for them. Believe me, this is the absolute truth. And this is especially why salespeople, who call on retailers, should be concentrating on what their proposal will GIVE that retailer or DO for that retailer, instead of how the product was made, or how its packed, or any of those other areas that are really more about the supplier or the product and not about the actual benefits that retailer will receive.

Look, as retailers, we are always trying to determine what kind of benefits we can receive out of every proposal that's presented to us. That's a major part of our job. So, when you sit down and start talking, we start analyzing each statement you make. We start visualizing possible benefits we could get if we agreed to your proposal. Now some retailers are better at this than others, but every retailer I know is trying to find benefits that will make them more profitable or better operators.

So, when you make the statement, …

"… this new product is packaged in 8oz. bags, 24 bags per case."

We will immediately start thinking and asking ourselves questions like …

> *… 8oz bags? Hmmm … that's too small for our regular shelves, but I wonder if it could drive some sales in my picnic section?*

> *… Maybe displaying them by the hot food to-go area, could drive some additional sales.*

> *… I wonder if that size would work by the checkout area?*

> *… what if we tried a Buy One Get One promotion, … buy a 16oz size and get this 8oz size free?*

And see, here's the point, the original statement, ***"this new product is packaged in 8oz. bags, 24 bags per case,"*** is not really a statement about benefits I receive, … instead, it's a statement about YOUR product. In fact, that actual statement doesn't help me at all, it is of no benefit to me, … BUT, … I'll take that statement and start trying to figure out a way that I can get a benefit out of what you're proposing.

In other words, we'll take that '8oz. bag' statement about **YOU** and try to determine if we could use it to benefit **US**. Retailers do this all the time because we're all trying to find that special promotion or concept that will generate more profit.

Now, once this concept is explained, the vast majority of salespeople I work with understand the need to make their presentations more retail oriented and to concentrate on the benefits their retailers will receive. But, I've also found many of these same salespeople have difficulty differentiating between an 'item' being a benefit to the retailer versus being a benefit to their company.

As an example, I've had sales reps tell me that the statement, …

'… our company is spending $3 million in advertising for next month's product launch' …

… would be a good example of a retail benefit. Now, from my perspective, as a retailer, this point is really about YOU, the manufacturer. You're spending the $3 million on advertising, … it has nothing to do with me. In fact, I really can't relate to this statement because I have no idea if this will effect me or my customers, … plus, even if I think there might be some effect, I don't know how much or if it's even worth my time. So in reality, the comment means very little to me, if anything, at all.

But, if you take that same comment, ('we're spending $3 million on advertising for next month's product launch,') and expand it to include a few extra points like, …

- … of which more than $1 million will be spent right here in your market

- … this whole media blitz starts in 8 weeks

- … we're projecting it will generate about $8 million in your market alone

- … and based on your market penetration, you're in position to grab almost $6 million of that, if we can get the displays up and the stores ready to go.

Okay, now you've given me something to think about, … you've tied YOUR information to something that's a benefit for ME, … <u>sales</u>. And, you're telling me that based on your projections, I'll receive a benefit of approximately $6 million in sales, if I can get my stores ready. See how this changes this initial statement from being about **YOU** (how much money YOU'RE spending on advertising) to about **ME** (how much sales I can get).

What usually happens, is the sales rep makes that initial statement (we're spending $3 million in the product launch), and then I'm left (as I explained before) to try and determine (1) if there's any kind of benefit to me, … (2) if there is, then how much, …. and (3) if the benefit is worth agreeing to your proposal.

The problem is, you really don't want your retailer having to break anything down to make it relevant. That's dangerous. Instead, you want to make sure I understand exactly what my benefits are. That means you should be breaking that $3 million national advertising concept down and explaining exactly why it's relevant, what my benefits will be and how much better my life will be because of it. Remember, retailers don't purchase products or services, … we purchase what we think those products or services will give us or do for us, … **we purchase the benefits.**

In this case, we would never agree to your program just because of a $3 million ad program, because that $3 million ad program, itself, means nothing to us, nothing! But, we very well might agree if you help us visualize the benefits we'll receive or get because of that ad program. That's really what I want to know. Remember, …

> **… it's not the $3 million ad program that's important, it's the benefits I'll receive because of that $3 million ad program, that's important.**

So, the key for manufacturers and their sales reps, is to remember, it's not about YOUR company, YOUR product or even how much money you're spending on YOUR promotion, ... instead, it's all about the BENEFITS, ... the BENEFITS I'll receive because of those things. That's why you should never leave it up to your retailer to try and determine what those benefits are, ... you need to make them the basis of your proposal.

Paint a picture of how much better off your retailer and his company will be by agreeing to your idea. It's really just that simple. So, maybe the real question I should be asking is, ...

"Just how good of a painter are you?"

QUESTIONS:

(Fill in the Blank) Retail buyers don't purchase products or services, ... they purchase _____
_____
_____.

Buck spends a good amount of time, in this chapter, talking about the need for sales reps to concentrate on the benefits their products and services provide, and not just the products or services themselves. Does you think this makes sense? Why or why not?

_____
_____
_____
_____
_____

Here are two statements a sales rep could make when trying to convince a retailer to agree to his proposal. What could you add to each comment to make it more relevant to the retailer's benefits, not the manufacturer's.

1) **"It comes in 8oz. bags packed 24 per case."**_____
_____
_____.

2) **"This week we've reduced it by $25 per case."**_____
_____
_____.

The last line of this chapter is **"Just how good of a painter are you?"** Explain what this question is about and why it's important.

_____
_____
_____
_____

CHAPTER V

WHY PILING UP THE BENEFITS IS ESSENTIAL

Okay, here's a bold statement!

As a retailer, I judge and value you and your products based on the benefits I receive from you and your products.

Does that make sense? You got it? Look, as a supplier, don't you value and rate us based on how many stores we have, … customers we have, … the total amount of sales we generate, etc.? Not sure? Well, ask yourself, would you rather have an 80-store chain agree to your proposal or a 9-store chain? That's not really a tough decision is it?

So why is this the case? Well, don't you believe the benefits you'll receive from the 80-store chain will be higher than in the 9-store operation? In fact, you can almost spend the same amount of time with both retailers, but the payback potential of the 80-store chain is 'out of sight' compared to the average 9-store operator.

Now, one of the interesting points most sales reps fail to grasp is that we retailers also value you and your products based on the benefits you provide us. It's really a very simple business relationship, the more benefits we gain by using your products and services, (help me build sales, add innovation, solve some of my problems, provide consumer data, etc.) the more we value you and your company.

So, in our workshops, we keep stressing, over and over, it's the BENEFITS that are really the key to your success.

The more benefits you can provide, ... in products, information, services and yourself, ... the more valuable you become, PERIOD!

It's really this simple!

Now, I've found once this concept is explained, most sales reps understand it, ... it makes sense and it's logical, ... but let me add one little point. I think it's easy to see the need to emphasize the benefits when you're presenting a proposal or making a presentation, ... but what about the benefits you're currently providing based on all of your products I'm carrying right now?

Do you think I still remember them all? Do you think you get 'credit' for all that you and your products are currently doing for me?

Now, these are critical questions because they deal with the current situation you're in, not something down the road. In other words, right now, at this exact minute, think of the retailer with whom you do the most business. Now, does that retailer understand and give you full credit for all of the benefits you are currently providing? Does your retailer recognize them?

This is really important because one of the basic truths of selling to retailers is, ...

... unless you keep reminding me of the benefits you're currently providing me, you'll lose them.

That's right, you'll lose them, because eventually I'll forget them and then, they just end up as part of all the every day muck!

BAM! Right away I can hear you saying, *"Muck? Muck? What in the world do you mean by 'every day muck'?"*

Well, I'm just referring to all of the stuff that goes on day after day, week after week, month after month and often just gets lost. It just becomes part of the process, it ends up as all of that normal, every day, nothing special, in the background, 'status quo,' stuff. As an example, when I agreed to put your products in my store, maybe you provided a piece of equipment to help display them. Initially, I think of that equipment as a benefit you provided, because it helps me achieve better sales, … but the longer that piece of equipment is there, the less and less of a benefit it becomes. And eventually, it just becomes part of the 'muck,' part of the normal everyday stuff, … it loses its significance, … that is, it loses its significance unless YOU keep reminding me of the benefits (sales, profits, etc.) I'm getting because that piece of equipment is still there. And that's exactly the role you have to play in this whole benefit scenario.

Look, as a typical buyer in today's marketplace, I see a minimum of 25 to 30 sales presentations a week. So realistically, why would you expect me to remember all of the benefits you're providing when I'm constantly dealing with all of the other products, as well as all of those other buying scenarios? I mean, really think about that for a minute, … and do you really want to leave all of that to chance?

One of my favorite sayings is …

… a person who doesn't read, loses his advantage over the person who never learned.

I really like this saying, and I believe it to be 100% true, … but, I don't think it stops there. In fact, I think this same analogy can be applied to sales reps calling on retailers, and it would go something like this …

> … if a sales rep doesn't continue to tell his retailer about the benefits of the products and services he is providing, sooner or later that retailer will forget, and then that sales rep loses any advantage over other companies who never provided those benefits in the first place.

Look, if your retailer forgets about any of the benefits you're currently providing him, then you lose them, … AND because of that, you lose any advantage you had over other companies that never provided those benefits in the first place. And believe me, … as a retailer, this is exactly what happens. And, it happens a lot more than you realize.

Not sure? Then how would you feel about doing this? Go to your two best retailers, right now, and ask them to tell you what benefits you and your company are currently providing. What do you think they would say? What kind of response would you get? How many benefits could they name? Now be honest with yourself, because obviously, there's no right answer, … it just comes down to what your retailer would say versus how many benefits you know you're providing.

Of course, if you're like most sales reps I work with, and your retailer is like most retailers I know, there will be a major difference between what you know you're providing and what the retailer recognizes, or gives you credit for providing. And that's the problem, because whether you realize it or not, you just lost any advantage you should have, by providing those benefits, over other companies that don't.

You see, I believe your job can't just be selling new programs, …

**… it also has to be continuing to reinforce
(1) the benefits of your programs and services
that I'm currently using, and
(2) the benefits you, personally, provide.**

These are critical elements to building your business. You can not allow your retailer to forget the benefits you are providing. Here's an example of why this is so important.

1) I've given you a certain amount of space in my store. That may include an end-of-aisle display, or a table, or a rack, or any number of facings. Each of those displays is currently generating a certain amount of sales and profits (benefits) for me.

2) I listen to 40 or more sales presentations each week, and every one of them wants me to give them additional space. In fact, I've never yet had a salesperson want to give space back to me. And the truth is, there is only a certain amount of space in my store, … so in reality, these salespeople want the space you've got.

3) Your space is always at risk. You've got to continually make sure your retailer knows the value, the benefits you're providing for each of your merchandising areas.

Remember, retailers aren't interested in the product itself, they're interested in the benefits they receive because of that product. So, you have to continually keep your retailer aware of what benefits each of your display areas is generating. You want the retailer to see the benefits of each display, not just the display itself. In other words, you want your retailer to look at that rack and see $1,300 per week in sales and $600 in profits, instead of just a metal rack. And this applies to each merchandising area: extra facings, a special display table, and on and on.

Of course, what traditionally happens is most salespeople don't start communicating about the current benefits a rack or a display generates until they lose that particular rack or display, ... and then they 'can't understand why it happened.'

And, although you probably don't want to hear it, if I forget the benefit that rack is providing, then as a salesperson, it's nobody's fault but your own. That's the way I look at it, ... it's your fault, not mine. If your products and/or services have certain retail benefits that distinguish your company from the others, and you allow your retailer to forget them or never be made aware of them, that's a disaster, a total disaster, ... and it's your fault because you've let this happen.

I'm sorry, but there's really no other way to look at it, ... the responsibility is yours ... PERIOD! The only saving grace to this situation is that it's not as uncommon as you might think. In fact, based on my experience, it's more the reality than the exception.

For some reason, the vast majority of sales reps I see, are guilty of exactly this situation. They don't continue to tell their retailers about the benefits of the products and/or services they're providing. For some reason, they seem to think that once a product is in a retailer, their job is over. They don't bring it up, ... they ignore it. Then, all of a sudden, somewhere down the line, that product gets removed, cut back or replaced and they're all upset.

Now, as a retailer, I've often wondered, why this happens. Has no one ever taken the time to explain how important this is? Do sales reps have a difficult time identifying what a benefit really is? Are they unsure and scared, or do they not know how to keep this information at the forefront of their conversations?

In reality, I guess the 'why' it's happening really doesn't matter. What's important is, as a sales rep, you need to keep reminding your retailer of the reasons he said "yes" to you in the first place, ... keep demonstrating to your retailer what a great decision that was by keeping him updated on the benefits your current products are providing, ... and above everything else, remember, this can be a 'game changer' for you and your company.

QUESTIONS:

(Fill in the Blanks)

The more benefits you can provide, the more _____ you become.

Unless you can keep reminding me of the benefits you're currently providing me, _____ them.

A person who doesn't read, loses their advantage over the person who _____ !

Whose fault does Buck say it is, if a retailer forgets about the benefits he's receiving from a certain group of products or a display? Please explain why you agree or disagree with his comment.

_____
_____
_____
_____
_____
_____
_____

In this chapter, Buck refers to something he calls "Muck." In fact, he says if a sales rep isn't careful, some of the benefits of his/her programs can end up in the muck! What is he talking about and why is this such a bad thing?

_____
_____
_____
_____
_____
_____
_____

This total chapter is really about one thing. In fact, Buck comments, "The more _____ you can provide, ... in products, information, services and yourself, ... the more valuable you become, PERIOD! What is this word, and why is it so important?

_____

_____

_____

_____

_____

_____

Chapter VI

WHAT VALUES DO YOU, PERSONALLY ADD?

Okay, here's a question I want to ask you. As a retailer, talking to you, as a salesperson, …

"What kind of value do you believe you, personally, add to your products or services?"

In other words, "If I called your office every month, and ordered enough of your product to take care of my stores, what would I NOT receive, what would I NOT get or what would I NOT experience because you weren't in the picture?" Or, maybe even a better way to look at this is, "Why do I need you?" "What do you add to the picture?" "What value do you bring to our business dealings?"

Now obviously, these are very important questions and maybe you think they're too personal, but truthfully, they get right to the heart of our business relationship. You see, anybody can show up at my office once a month, … anybody can take an order from me or deliver a deal sheet, … but that kind of person doesn't add value to anything. In fact, if that's who you are, then I'd rather you just send me your new deal or price every month by email. That way I don't even have to schedule any time with you and that will make my life much easier.

For me, and the retailers I work with today, expect more from our sales reps. We believe, …

> **… it's your job to show us how using your products or services will help solve some of our problems or help us reach some of our objectives.**

If you don't do that, if you leave that piece up to us, you've missed the whole reason for your existence as a sales person. And, it amazes me how often this simple concept is missed. Plus, since I've never been the kind of person to keep my mouth shut, I seem to get myself into a lot of trouble.

To prove my point, I remember years ago participating in a retail discussion panel at one of the major annual supermarket conferences. Our topic was **"Brokers, and How They Can Help Retailers!"** There were five of us on the retail panel and our job was to answer questions from the moderator and then the audience about Brokers in general. I knew most of the retailers on this panel, as these were people from the major chains and we had met and talked at previous national conventions.

Now, like most large conference panel discussions, the participants are asked to show up the night before to check out the set-up and basically get a chance to feel comfortable with the total surroundings. As we reviewed how things would go the following day, the five of us began discussing how we felt about brokers and some of the issues each of us we were facing.

Without exception, at this particular time, each one of us was having major problems with the brokers in our areas.

This included everything from brokers not showing up, or not calling for orders, to no program assistance, not getting product on time and lack of contact with their principals. In short, none of us were happy with what was going on, and quite honestly, I left that 'test run' really excited about the pertinent discussion I thought we'd have at the next day's panel discussion.

So how did it turn out? Well, when it came time for the retail panel, the main hall was filled, standing room only. Then the lights went down and the moderator was introduced. She said a few words and then brought each of us out on the stage with a brief introduction. Once we all were seated, I was in the fourth position from the moderator, she announced she would open the discussion by having each of us give a short overview of the broker situation in our own area.

She then turned to my friend from one of the national chains, let's call him Jim, as he was the closest to her on her left, and she asked him to comment about the broker situation in his area. I immediately thought, *"good, now we'll get some of these important issues out in the open right away."* The night before, Jim had been one of the most vocal about how bad the brokers were in his area so I felt he'd really help to get this discussion moving, … but, that's not quite the way it went.

Instead, Jim, said something like, *"You know, we have some of the finest brokers in the country in our area, and it's a pleasure dealing with them. In fact, we wouldn't be able to serve our customers, as well as we do, without the effort and commitment these people have made to our business. There's no doubt they are an essential part of our total business dealings."* Then he stopped.

Now, I sat there stunned, yep stunned. This wasn't even close to what he had talked about the

night before. I couldn't believe what had just happened.

But, I'm sorry to say, it was only the beginning because the next retailer followed right along. He commented, *"Look, I have to agree with what Jim just said. We too have some of the best brokers I've seen, working with us. It's good to know they are so committed to us and our consumers. Truthfully, we wouldn't be in business today without them."*

Oh, My God! I was sitting there going bananas. And as the third retailer echoed the same sentiments about how good the brokers were in his area and how much he depended on them, I leaned over to another friend of mine, who was on my left, and said,

"You better hang on to your hat, because I think what I'm going to say may really upset this place."

Now we had known each other for at least 5 years and I considered him a good friend. I saw him grimace, shake his head a little, then smile and say, *"Oh, brother, here we go!"*

So, in essence, the three retailers before me all talked about how great the brokers were in their area, … and how essential they had been to their business and how there was no way they could get along without them. Then it was my turn. And I still remember clearing my throat, while my mind was racing as to exactly what I should say.

Now, have you ever been in a situation like that? You know, the kind of situation where once those first words come out of your mouth, there's no going back, … you're committed. It's like that conversation you have with your girlfriend when you want to break up. You can't start off by saying, "I think we ought to see other people," and then change your mind and say, "I was only kidding." Nope, once you start, that's it, there's no going back.

So here I am, … all of these thoughts racing through my mind! Should I just follow the others and adopt the party line, or should I really open up about the issues I was facing? I swallowed hard, thought MAYBE when I got back home I'd actually break up with my girlfriend, and then I began with the following statement.

"You know, I'm really thrilled to be here today, because I've been wondering where all of the good brokers in this country were located, … **and now I know, they're all in your areas, because they certainly aren't in mine."**

Now, I don't know how many of you have actually been in a room filled with people and heard the room itself gasp? Yeah, that's right, the room, not just the people in it, because that's exactly what happened. When I

made that statement, I swear you could actually hear the room gasp, … it came out of the darkness. I figured it must have been hiding in the walls or the ceilings or someplace, I don't exactly know where, … but it must have been trapped there for a while, because once I made that statement, it rushed out and encompassed the whole crowd in some kind of green-like fog. Well, to me it looked like a green fog, but I admit, I was under a lot of stress. Anyway, that gasp really startled me, and then everything, and I mean everything, went quiet, deadly quiet.

It was at that exact point I actually decided that when I got back home, I WOULD definitely break up with my girlfriend, ... and then the moderator said, *"Well, Buck, what kind of problems are you experiencing?"* And that was all it took, as I opened up about the same things our group had been talking about the night before. I quickly rattled off two major issues, and was starting the third when the moderator stopped me and said maybe it was best to hear from the last retailer on the panel.

Now, once each of us made our initial remarks, the floor was opened, and audience members were allowed to write comments or questions on 3x5 cards that were then brought up on stage to the moderator. For the rest of the hour, there were only two questions directed to someone besides me or that didn't pertain to my opening comments. I got accused of saying, "I hate brokers" ... "that we shouldn't have brokers," ... "that I'll never use a broker," and on and on.

It got so bad, even a few of the other retailers started protecting me with comments about how they were experiencing some of the same situations I had mentioned. Of course, I also noticed the retailer on my right and my friend on my left had both

moved their chairs a little away from me. *(I guess they didn't want to get hit when the audience started throwing rotten tomatoes.)* Anyway, it really didn't make a difference what any of the other retailers said, it was too late, no one was listening to them, the room had already gasped, and I was the culprit.

Finally, after what seemed like a 3-hour marathon (this was only supposed to be an hour panel), the moderator said it was time to end the discussion. She thanked everyone for their "enthusiastic" participation, *(Yeah, she actually used the word 'enthusiastic.')* then turned to me and asked if I had anything else I wanted to add. Again, here I was at the crossroads, do I just say no, and try to sneak out of the place, go back to the hotel and take a shower *(I could actually feel the sweat running down the middle of my back)*, or do I actually make one last effort knowing I may have to fight my way out. *(Plus, although it was never confirmed, I could have sworn someone had actually draped a hangman's noose over one of the crossbeams in the back of the room. Yeah, I'm sure I saw it swinging back there.)* Well, I decided to make it two for two, so I ended the session this way.

Didn't I tell you I play golf on Thursdays so I need your order by noon?

"Look, I didn't say I dislike brokers, in fact there are two or three that I deal with on a regular basis that I consider as partners in my business. We work together and I respect what they do and who they are. But there's another group of brokers that seem to feel they're owed the 3¢ to 5¢ they get on every pound of product I buy, just because they represent the client that I happen to want to buy from. They don't help me one bit, they don't come up with promotional ideas. They don't try to find ways to increase my business. I rarely ever see them.

They are a non-entity in my business. In fact, one of the major brokers in my area actually told me, to my face, that I had to have any orders in to him by noon on Thursdays because he plays golf on Thursday afternoon, and takes Fridays off."

"Now, that sounds like a pretty good job to me. So, why does this guy

get 4¢ on every pound of product I buy, when all he does, is turn around and call that order in to the manufacturer? I mean, I'd rather call the order directly into the manufacturer myself, and take the 4¢ reduction on our end."

"I believe, and I don't care who you are, an employee in our stores, a manufacturer's sales rep, and yes, even a broker, … if you don't add value to the products you represent, then, I'm sorry, but you don't deserve the money you get paid. To me, it's just that simple." And with that, the moderator cut off the bright spotlight she'd brought up on stage to shine in my eyes, and ended the discussion. *(Okay, I'm kidding about the spotlight part.)*

Now, as soon as we got off stage *(My legs were wobbling so badly, I almost stumbled as I began looking for a back-stage exit),* the other retailers gathered around me and were laughing, congratulating me for my comments and talking about how they never expected me, even though they felt the same way, to say the things I had. Even the moderator came over and talked about how, *"this was one panel discussion where no audience member got up and walked out early. They all wanted to hear and see what was going to happen next." (I actually think they just stayed to see if I was going to be lynched or not, … I heard Vegas had the odds at 2 to 1, … and those odds weren't in my favor.)*

At that moment, as I was looking for a back-stage exit where I could make a quick escape, I saw two brokers I work with come through the crowd and head over toward me. One of them had his hand in his coat pocket, which concerned me some, (Can you carry a concealed gun in Chicago?), but as they approached they both were laughing, so I relaxed a little. They held out their hands for me to shake and I was glad to see that because I was also concerned they might be the committee sent to drag me to that noose. *(Did I mention I saw a noose swaying back and forth in the back of the room? I really did!)*

Anyway, then they commented how wonderful the whole thing went. They said once the brokers around them found out they were from my area, they got all kinds of condolences and comments about how terrible it must be to have me as their main retailer and so on and so on. I heard later these two guys didn't have to buy a drink for the rest of the conference. Other brokers felt so sorry for them that they kept their glasses filled the whole time. Of course, no one bought me drinks, *(I don't know if I would have felt safe drinking it if they had),* but it didn't stop there.

In fact, by the time, two days later, I returned to my office, my buyers had already been told about my comments from some of the sales reps that called on them. They thought it was great. Anyway, for at least the next year or so, I got references to this panel discussion over and over again. Retailers would comment about how it was about time someone really spoke up about the broker problems, while often, I'd hear from sales people about how I hate brokers, don't want to do business with them, and wanted my manufacturers to get rid of their broker companies, and on and on.

Now, I apologize if I've gotten somewhat carried away talking about this conference panel on brokers, but I feel the same way about sales reps as I do brokers, ... or anyone else for that matter. If you don't add value to the products or services you're representing, then why should I listen to you, ... why should I even spend time with you?

As a retailer, this was something I preached over and over to our stores' employees. To me, increasing the value you personally add to your product and service offerings is the best way to set yourself apart from your competition. Why? The main reason is because it can't be duplicated, ... it's yours. And this same philosophy applies directly to sales reps. If you're not adding value to the products or services you're representing, then all I've got to make my buying determination on is the product or service itself, and the price. And quite honestly, products and services can be copied and prices can always be beat.

Look, one of the great truths about sales is ...

> **... the better YOU are at adding value to your products, the less 'price' becomes a buying qualifier.**

This is so true, ... but it also means, if all your retailer wants is a better price, then what does that say about your ability to add value to your products? In other words, if price is the only issue for your retailer, then it must mean he doesn't recognize any of the other things you do as a benefit. That's not good, so right now, I'd like you to think about how you would answer the following questions.

"What kind of value do you add to your products?

**"What unique benefits do I gain by having
YOU calling on me?"**

Do YOU *(check all that apply)* add value because of your ...

o   ... level of product, service or industry knowledge?

o   ... ability to develop special merchandising programs?

o   ... ability to position programs to help me reach my objectives
or solve some of my problems?

o   ... ability to explain the product's quality and how my customers
want it?

o   ... ability to explain how your service will make my life easier
or more productive?

o   ... ability to make solid sales and profit projections?

o   ... ability to ask questions to determine my needs and objectives?

o   ... willingness to keep me on track and make my program
goals?

o   ... willingness to bring me ideas you see in other markets?

o   ... willingness to listen to my needs and try to help solve them?

o   ... awareness of the changing marketplace and what consumers
want today?

o   ... awareness of my company's weaknesses and strengths?

Now, based on the points you marked, look at the ways you're currently adding value to your products. This is really important, because this is what shows 'your worth,' … this is what shows 'your value.' But, also take the time to observe the points you didn't mark. These represent the numerous opportunities you have available to increase your worth, to increase your value.

So remember, if you're not adding value to the products and services you represent, then from your company's perspective, you're not really doing what you're paid to do, … and from my perspective, as a retailer, I really don't see a need to spend any time with you.

But, if you're looking for ways to add value, then don't forget …

1. … the value you add, must be considered a value by me, the retailer. I'm the judge as to whether it's a value or not, … and the judge as to how great a value it may be.

2. … the more value you can add to the products and services you represent, the more worth you have as a sales rep to me, to your company, and most important of all, to yourself.

So take a look at how much value you bring to the deal, and make it a point to continually search for ways to increase it.

Remember, the more value you bring, the bigger benefit you are to me, and the more valuable you are to your company.

QUESTIONS:

This chapter deals with the 'values you personally' add to your products or services. Buck says that, 'it's part of your job to show retailers how using your products or services will help solve some of their problems." This seems like a big responsibility. Do you agree or disagree and why do you feel this way.

_____

_____

_____

_____

Buck also comments that one of the great truths about sales is, **the better you are at adding value to your products, the less "price' becomes a buying qualifier**. Have you found this to be true? Why or why not?

_____

_____

_____

_____

In this chapter, there's a list of 12 "Values" a sales rep can use to distinguish themselves. You were asked to mark the ones you use today. Please select two of the 'values' you did **NOT** mark, … write them here, … and then list a few things you could do to begin including them in your overall sales strategy.

1. _____

_____

_____

2. _____

_____

_____

CHAPTER **VII**

ARE THERE TIMES WHEN YOU SHOULDN'T BE SELLING?

Okay, here's a question for you …

"Do you have a friend, next door neighbor or maybe it's a relative who always seems to be wanting something every time they show up?"

Do you know someone like that? And maybe it's even gotten to the point where every time you see them you immediately start wondering, *"Okay, what is it now?"* Have you got a situation like that?

Well, for me, it's a relative I'll call, Uncle Bob. *(Now of course, that isn't his real name, and maybe for you it's an Aunt Nancy, but if any relative of mine read this Chapter, they'd know right away whom Uncle Bob was.)* I never hear from Uncle Bob unless he needs something. It may be money, it may be to help him move *(he's done it three times now)*, it may be a particular situation he's in and needs someone to help him get out, … but make no mistake, it's always something.

So, here's my question … "how do you feel when you pick up the phone and hear your Uncle Bob's voice? I mean, what kind of thoughts start running through your head? Do you feel good when you recognize his voice on the phone or do you get that sick little feeling in your stomach? Okay, maybe you get that **BIG** sick feeling in your stomach!"

Now, I'd like you to consider these two thoughts for a moment, ... first, do you think it's possible that thoughts like those could be running through retailers' heads every time another salesperson starts one of their "guess what I've got for you" sales pitches? I mean, think about how many of these 'presentations' we each see every week, every month. So, the minute a sales rep starts another typical 'guess what I've got for you' kind of approach, is it possible we could be thinking, "Oh brother, here we go again"? Well, I'm here to tell you ... Yes, oh most definitely, Yes!

Okay? Now the second thought I'd like you to consider is, if this is your typical approach and this is the kind of 'stuff' you bring to me, could I be dreading seeing YOU come through MY door? Is my first thought, "Oh no, here he is again." Or maybe a better question to ask is, ...

... are YOU, my Uncle Bob?

Wow! Now that's a frightening thought isn't it? And how do you know if you are or you aren't? I mean, your retailer isn't really going to tell you, ... after all, I've never told my Uncle Bob how I feel, ... I just put up with him. So is it possible certain retailers are just 'putting up' with you?

Obviously I don't know your specific situations but I do know if the truth actually came out, there would be a lot of surprised sales reps out there named Bob.

So, let me quickly address two specific points about this Uncle Bob scenario.

POINT ONE: There are certain salespeople out there right now, whom I feel the same about, as I do my Uncle Bob. It doesn't make any difference how long it has been, I still dislike listening to their same old tired sales pitches. Man, don't they ever improve? So, Help! Please, just hurry up, give me your pitch and get out of my office! Then, at least I won't have to see you again until next month!

Let me in, I'm Bob, your next appointment!

So yes, there are sales reps out there just like that, ... and hopefully, you aren't one of them.

AND HERE'S POINT TWO: As a buyer, I can see six to eight sales people a day, five days a week, fifty weeks a year. And that means each individual time, I have to gear up, get my game face on, be ready to hear a proposal, make some type of decision and then relay that decision *(most of the time 'No')* to the salesperson. And the truth is, whether I like the salesperson or not, ... I still have to go through that 'get ready, gear up, it's business' process each and every time.

But, here's what's really telling about these kind of selling scenarios, ... there have been situations when I've had a salesperson walk in *(Remember, I've got my game face on and I'm ready to rumble)* and he'll say something like, ...

"... Buck, I'm not here to sell you anything today, I just wanted to talk about ... ."

Now, he may want to talk about last week's ad plan, or something that's going on with their company, ... but it doesn't make any difference, because when that "I'm not here to sell you anything" comment comes out, I can immediately sense myself relaxing. All of a sudden I don't feel like I have to be so focused, ... I don't have to be so 'on guard,' ... I don't have to be so 'you salesperson, me retailer' type of relationship. Instead, I can just relax a little and be me with no other agenda.

So here's my first point, ... **you don't want me to think of you as Uncle Bob, a person always wanting something, always pushing.**

Yes, you're the salesperson and I'm the retailer, but you want me to think of you as more of a consultant, someone that's there to help me instead of someone that's only looking for their next sale.

That brings us to my second point, ...

... some of your calls on me shouldn't be sales calls.

That's right, they shouldn't be sales calls, ... instead, we should be talking about last month's promotion. How did it go? ... Were we successful? ... How successful were we? We should be discussing our upcoming company plans and you should be telling me about your company's plans, too. We should be looking at possible problem areas which you may be able to help me solve. Plus, do you have any data that would help me key-in on certain consumer demographic groups?

These are all important areas because by taking the time to discuss them, you're demonstrating to me that you're interested in more than just how much product you can move on your next promotion. We're talking business here, … and reviewing ways which you can help me. You become more than just an order-taker or a deal-deliverer, … you're separating yourself from the other 6 or 7 people I'll see today or the other 30 or more people I'll see this week.

Think about this for a minute. Can you see how this puts you in a different light, … moves you to a different level compared to all of the other Uncle Bob salespeople? That's why this is so important.

Okay? Now, one more point. Even though we're talking business, you are still selling! That's right, you're still selling. You may not be selling a product, … you may not be selling a promotional idea … you may not even be selling a marketing plan, … but you are most definitely selling. And what are you selling?

You are selling yourself and the value you represent in our relationship. And quite honestly, you'll find that …

… selling yourself and the value you bring to me and my company is much more important than selling any particular product you've got.

Remember, the more you can act as a consultant, a confidant or an advisor, the closer and closer you move to being on my side of the desk, where we become allies working together. But, if you're always trying to get that next sale, that next promotion, that next item placement, … then more often than not, we'll remain adversaries sitting on opposite sides of that desk.

So, to wrap up this thought, here are the last two questions I have for you:

First, when you come through that office door, ... how do your retailers think of you? Do they regard you as their Uncle Bob (the "oh brother, here he is again" scenario), ... or are you actually a 'welcomed' addition to their family?

And second, when you come through that door, ... are you always

trying to sell them another product, another promotion, another whatever, ... or have you learned how to sell the advantages YOU bring to them, by talking about their business and helping them with the problems they're facing?

Now, this may sound strange coming from a retailer, ... but take it from me, as far as business calls are concerned, ... you'll do much better if you aren't always selling product, promotions or programs.

Look, I'll never admit I said this, *(that's why these next couple of sentences, printed in vanishing ink, will disappear less than 5 minutes after you read them)* but the biggest advantage you have in any sales call, is yourself.

You are the difference maker!

That's why you should **ALWAYS** be selling me on the benefits and value you bring to our business relationship.

SELL ME on how smart you are, …

SELL ME on how much you know about my business, …

SELL ME on how you can help address my problems …

SELL ME on how YOU are the best business partner

a retailer could ask for, …

Sell Me, on YOU!

QUESTIONS:

Do you have a neighbor or a relative that's like Uncle Bob? What is it about this person that makes him your Uncle Bob?

_____

_____

_____

_____

_____

When you go in to see your retailers, are you always wanting something from them? Be honest. How do you think your retailers perceive you? Please explain why you feel this way.

_____

_____

_____

_____

_____

When was the last time you actually went in to see your retailer and only wanted to talk, get information, or share ideas?

_____

_____

_____

_____

_____

Buck says he believes that selling yourself and the value you bring to your retailer are even more important than selling a particular product? Please explain why you agree or disagree.

_____

_____

_____

_____

_____

FINAL THOUGHTS

As I said at the beginning, I've been in this industry a long time and one of the points that used to frustrate me the most was the fact that ...

... most of the sales reps who called on me, had very little understanding of the retailer side of the business, ... they really didn't understand who they were selling to.

And, at the same time, ...

... almost every retailer I knew would be happy to work closely with their sales rep counterparts, if they believed those reps truly wanted to help them be successful.

So, it was a problem then, and it's still one of the major problems today, ... retailers are willing to work closely with their sales reps, if they believe those reps truly care about them and want to help them be successful, and yet, most sales reps have no idea of how the retail business works and what retailers need in order to be successful.

For me, this booklet is a beginning, a first step on the journey of helping manufacturing sales reps, develop a better understanding of their retailers' needs.

And I hope, as you went through it, you were able to pick up a couple of points you can use to improve your relationship and sales opportunities with your retailers.

You see, I still believe the more you understand the needs of your retailers, the more your sales presentations will become aligned with those needs, and that will result in better programs for your retailers and more 'yeses' for your proposals.

So YES, retailers and manufacturers can work together!

Good luck with your selling, and maybe we'll get a chance to meet somewhere down the line. I'd like that.

Buck

Buck Jones
A Buck's Worth
(469) 644-8202

ABOUT THE AUTHOR

Buck, an experienced leader and international consultant with expertise in retail and manufacturing, spent over 25 years as a retailer, starting out as a part-timer while in high school, and ending up as a corporate Vice President for one of the largest grocery companies in the U.S. He formed his own company in the early 90's and has been working with manufacturers and retailers in the U.S., Brazil and Europe ever since.

As an acclaimed trainer and educator, he developed and managed a retail training program used by more than 1,600 supermarkets for over ten years, … as a speaker, he's a member of the National Speakers Association and has been featured on almost every retail platform in the country, … and as an author, he wrote his own column for *Progressive Grocer Magazine,* for a six year period, and this is his second book.

Visit his website at …
www.abucksworth.com

Follow him at …
www.linkedin.com/in/buck-jones-8b51201/
www.facebook.com/mybucksworth

Or contact him at …
**A Buck's Worth • 190 E Stacy Rd #306-273
Allen, TX 75002 • (469) 644-8202**